Expanded Edition
Now with a Selection of Psalms Verses

Infusing Hope, Inspiring Action

A Daily Psalms Journal for Women

Janita Pavelka

Infusing Hope, Inspiring Action:
A Daily Psalms Journal for Women
Expanded Edition
by Janita Pavelka

Unless otherwise identified, Scripture quotations are taken from
THE HOLY BIBLE, NEW INTERNATIONAL VERSION®, NIV®.
Copyright © 1973, 1978, 1984, 2010 by Biblica, Inc.™
www.xulonpress.com. Emphasis within Scripture quotations
is the author's own.

Janitapavelka.com
janitapavelka@gmail.com

Book Design by Sara Mahalek
www.mahalekcreative.com

Editing by Kristine Jacobson
www.krjpr.com

ISBN-13: 978-1981442195
ISBN-10:1981442197
Printed in the USA

DEDICATION

For my piano teachers,
Mrs. Buechler, Mrs. Hall and Neil Moore,
Who (helped) train my hands for war
And my fingers for battle
(Psalm 144:1)

CONTENTS

INTRODUCTION

This journal is for you, dear one.
It is meant to catapult you into the arms of your loving Savior
so He can let you know how special and loved you are.
Give yourself permission to take time for yourself, to nurture
your spirit and soul, and to bask in God's love for you.

Did you know?

He loves you beyond comprehension, for as high as the heavens are above the earth, so great is His love toward you. (Psalms 103:11)
He delights in you and rejoices over you with singing. (Zephaniah 3:17)
He has so much to show you, tell you, and whisper to you. (1 Kings 19:12)
He is jumping up and down with glee that you are embarking on this journey of love, seeking His pure, unblemished love just for you! (John 3:16)
He has been waiting since your conception to be this intimate with you. (Jeremiah 1:5)

He is standing with open arms, excited and ready to go on a new love adventure with you daily. (1 Corinthians 16:23)
So sit back, rest in His arms, and bask in His adoration of you. Are you convinced yet that He has something exceptional waiting just for you?

This book walks you through the art of journaling. If you make journaling a vital part of your everyday life, it can pave the way to being more spiritually-minded, productive, organized, grateful, goal-oriented, creative, meditative, and a dreamer of dreams. Eventually you will get to the point where you desire it like you crave wholesome food, or sweet fellowship with a bestie, or a lavender bath, or an early-to-bed night with a riveting book, or a vigorous walk outside. Journaling slows you down, has you search your inner thoughts and listen as you ask the Lord what He wants to teach you each day. Life moves too quickly, and if we don't take enough time to quiet ourselves and tune into the Lord for His guidance, we may miss the shortcut God has for us. The daily discipline, the set aside time, and the gift of journaling will change your life. May you profoundly experience the importance of getting your thoughts out on paper and quieting your soul, like a weaned child on her Mother's lap. (Psalms 131:2) You will become a richer, deeper person because of the daily practice.

This practice of journaling and daily prayer is not meant to add to the "should pile" in your life. It is meant to set you free, as you shall know the Truth and the Truth will set you free. (John 8:32) Journaling is not meant to add a heavy burden to your life, or to put a yoke upon you, as Jesus says when you are yoked to Me, your weary soul will find rest. (Matthew 11:28-30) Implementing the art of journaling means absolutely NO perfectionism is allowed, nor any self-condemnation, for there is no shame or condemnation for those who are in Jesus Christ. You can just be who God created you to be as God is full of grace. He is longing for your attention and not concerned with your performance. Your journaling doesn't have to be done morning and night. Every blank doesn't need to be filled out completely with every "t" crossed and every "i" dotted. Man looks on the outer appearance, but God looks on the heart. (1 Samuel 16:7) He is not looking at your behavior; He cares about the healing of your heart, which produces lasting growth in your life.

This journal's purpose is multi-faceted. You will record your dreams, gratitude, verses, prayer requests, goals, risks, self-care, meditations, love for self and others, do overs, God's Truths about you, and God's messages from the Psalms, in short morning and evening entries. You will be more relaxed, optimistic and kinder, have improved sleep and productivity, and be more likely to attain your goals because of journaling and meditating on God's Word early in the morning and as the last event at night.

What is going to make you more successful in journaling?

The key to success will be guarding your bedtime. Did you know the new day starts in the evening? Therefore we need to start prepping for the next day at night. A solid bedtime routine sets you up to have a great day. The new day starts at sundown. According to Genesis 1:5, "God called the light "day," and the darkness he called "night." And there was evening, and there was morning--the first day." View it as a treat to go to bed early to savor your nightly wrap-up with God as He feeds your soul as you sleep. At night, you will be able to journal about how you loved others, loved yourself, tangible ways God demonstrated His love toward you, goals for tomorrow, forgiveness of self and others, and loving thoughts from God before bed. Before you were even born, all the days were ordained for you and written down before one of them came to be. (Psalms 139:16) You can face the new day with eagerness and anticipation of what He has established for you before the foundations of the earth. (Ephesians 1:4) Make every day the best day of your life!

Why use the Psalms for your daily meditation?

King David was a man after God's own heart. (I Samuel 13:14) Do you desire to be a woman after God's own heart? I do! What if you knew you could be more like Jesus by the end of this three-month journal? What if this book came with a "money back guarantee" that it would make you into a "woman after God's own heart" or a full refund? Do you believe it? Will you trust the God of the Universe, the One who formed you in your mother's womb, that He can change you from the inside out? Will you let Him have His way in your life? Will you commit to this challenge, just as you would commit to training for a big race? Yes, you will be changed spiritually, and it will spill over into your physical being, your relationships and your purpose in life. Will you devote three months to see that sort of change in your life? They will pass anyway, so why not apply the daily discipline of journaling and reap the fruit at the end of it?

Meditating on the Psalms, which is Hebrew poetry, helps you to know God better. The 150 Psalms are mainly laments, hymns, or songs of Thanksgiving. King David wrote half of the Psalms as an expression of his heart as a musician, king, warrior and shepherd. Almost every emotion is expressed in the Psalms, which gives us permission to be honest with our feelings and not hide them from God or ourselves.

A lament is a deep grief, sadness, expressing great sorrow or regret. If you read Psalm 22, the one Jesus quoted from the cross, you hear Him cry out to the Father, which gives us the license and the privilege to do the same. All of us face sorrows in life, such as: a loss of a loved one, a broken heart over our children's choices, a painful marriage or a divorce, infertility, abusive relationships, a loss of a job, the effects of slander, betrayal, suicide or suicidal thoughts, a terrible illness or a tragic financial loss. We all feel deep grief, sorrow or regret at times. Just like the days and seasons are cyclical, so is our sorrow and grief. Weeping lasts for the night, but joy comes in the morning. (Psalms 30:5)

Hymns are the second most common type found in the Psalms. Psalms means praise. In our morning journal time, we are praising the Lord by reading the Psalms, and we are praying as Psalms also means prayers. We sing hymns, which can be centuries old, in public or private, which are based on Scripture.

We also sing songs of thanksgiving, the third type in the Psalms, which go hand-in-hand with gratitude. Morning and night, we give gratitude and thanksgiving to God for the blessings in our lives, which emanate from Him, the Giver of Good Gifts. We recognize He is the Giver and we are the receiver, which brings humility into our lives. We are nothing, have nothing and can do nothing without the Lord. He is the One who makes our lives prosperous and full of meaning.

King David was God's musician, as he could not live without praise, and he praised with abandon. He was compelled to worship because it flowed out of his heart, and he is an example for many. The throng would line the streets to watch him sing and dance. Some folks wanted to join him, but couldn't because of fear or shame. Some didn't want to join him and judged him a fool. And some were not worried about what other people thought, but took the plunge and joined him. They were blessed because they stepped out in childlike faith and trusted the Messiah as their best dance partner. Learn to praise the Lord with abandon through immersing yourself in the Psalms.

Will you be one who focuses on Who is in control and not on how life will be? Will you value your vertical relationship with the Lord more than your horizontal ones? Will you let go of trying to be perfect, in control of your life and the lives of others, and let God take you on an amazing adventure of deep love?

As King David penned in Psalms 139: 7-12,
"Where can I go from your Spirit?
Where can I flee from your presence?
If I go up to the heavens, you are there;
if I make my bed in the depths, you are there.
If I rise on the wings of the dawn,
if I settle on the far side of the sea,
even there your hand will guide me,
your right hand will hold me fast.
If I say, "Surely the darkness will hide me
and the light become night around me,
even the darkness will not be dark to you;
the night will shine like the day, for darkness is as light to you."

Blessings on you, my dear one, as you experience God's never-ending love. May you know the depth and length and breadth and height of God's love for you. (Ephesians 3:18)

Lovingly,
Janita Pavelka
August 2017

HOW TO USE THIS JOURNAL

If you set aside 15 to 20 minutes in the morning and evening to quiet your mind and heart to listen to the Father, He has promised something special for you.

Morning Meditations

At the top of the page, write today's date and the Psalm for the day. Use your journal to praise, to pray, to give thanks, to write the dreams God places in your mind and heart, to express emotions, to confess the Truths about God, to accomplish your goals, to take risks, to take care of yourself daily, to love others and yourself, to forgive yourself, to wait on the Lord for answers, and to meditate on God's Truths about you.

How do you meditate? You focus on one bite-size truth for the day. Sit quietly, breathe slowly, and focus on one truth. Ask for a picture of you and Jesus sitting in a certain chair, or on a swing under a tree, or laying in the grass, or having a tea party in the garden, and plant the "happy place with Jesus" in your head. It will help you focus on your personal relationship with your Heavenly Father and what He has for you today.

Dreams

As soon as possible after waking up, write down your dreams as God speaks to us in dreams. Every dream may not have a message, but "even at night God speaks to our heart." (Psalms 16:7) If you cannot remember your night dreams, you can record your daydreams, or the dreams that God has placed in your heart. He wants us to dream.

Thoughts & Emotions

Feel free to write down your morning's thoughts and emotions as soon as possible. The plaguing thoughts and emotions can be carried into your day if you do not "dump" them on to the page. They can burrow themselves in your subconscious and wreak havoc if not released. The more you acknowledge and record your feelings, the more honest you become.

Gratitude

A heart that is grateful changes your whole world view. Every morning and every evening thank God for the good in your life. We all can find blessings, even in the worst of circumstances. In her wonderful book, *The Hiding Place*, Corrie ten Boom and her sister Betsie were thankful to God for lice because it kept the Nazi guards away from their sleeping quarters. If Corrie can be thankful for lice while being in a concentration camp in World War II, we can find things to be thankful for daily.

Psalms Messages

Choose a Psalms passage to read from the back of this book each day. Select which of the three categories you would like to use that day and tick the box to help with organization. This journal is not meant to put another yoke upon you, but to free your spirit to hear from God daily. Some journaling is better than no journaling, so set yourself up for success. The Holy Spirit is our constant Guide, and is the key when meditating on the Scriptures. Just ask Him, "What do you want me to learn from this passage, Lord?" and "Show me how to apply this to my life." James 1:23-25 says, "Anyone who listens to the Word but does not do what it says is like someone who looks at his face in a mirror and, after looking at himself, goes away and immediately forgets what he looks like. But whoever looks intently into the perfect law (teachings) that gives freedom, and continues in it—not forgetting what they have heard, but doing it—they will be blessed in what they do." Therefore we meditate on the Word and apply it to our lives. This is not a time of self-condemnation, for "there is therefore now no condemnation to them which are in Christ Jesus, who walk not after the flesh, but after the Spirit." (Romans 8:1) We simply ask how it applies to us, let the Lord speak, then listen and obey. We will never do it perfectly, so just relax and apply it in a child-like manner, because we all are on a learning curve, which He understands, and still adores us. God is Love, so His approach is always loving and kind.

Prayers

Everyone needs prayer, so we record prayer requests daily. Petitions can be for our families, our friends, our neighbors, our region, our world, and us. It builds our faith muscles when we see God answer. We already know God hears as 1 John 5:14-15 says, "This is the confidence we have in approaching God: that if we ask anything according to His will, He hears us. And if we know that He hears us — whatever we ask — we know that we have what we asked of Him." Write down your pleas, no matter how silly or how small. God hears them and loves it when we share our intimate thoughts with Him. He already knows our hearts, so He is not surprised, worried, disappointed or appalled with us. Recording your prayer requests is another facet of enjoying intimacy with Him.

Risk Today

You might think, "Why is this a daily category?" "What do risks have to do with the Psalms?" A common theme with the dying is they wished they had lived bigger lives, not so planned and secure. What dreams do you have? What wishes? What long-held, cherished ideas? What puts you out of your comfort zone? What gives you that 'butterflies in the stomach' feeling? Just ask God; He will show you the desires of your heart. (Psalms 34:7) It may be a phone call, a letter, a new business or ministry idea, expressing your true feelings, talking to a stranger, making new friendships, a trip, a thank-you note in the mail, or writing a book. Once you give yourself permission to dream, and act on it with daily little risks, the floodgates will open. It forces you to grow each day, which helps you live out your destiny.

Fundies (Fundamentals)

We all need more self-care in our lives. It needs to be the main focus of our daily life to be healthy, serve others and live a long, full life on this earth. There are three fundamentals that bring balance, longevity, energy and freedom into your life: eat, move, and sleep.

Eat: You need to eat nutrient-dense, whole foods, as close to nature as possible. Food that gives you life and doesn't rob you. Food that is real, not something concocted in a lab. (See Michael Pollan's *Food Rules* for a quick, but powerful read on the subject.)

Move: We all need more movement throughout the day. Sitting is hard on the body, and we need to schedule frequent motion during the day. Moving our body gives us energy, elongates our life, elevates our mood, helps with weight control, saves us money as we don't need as many trips to the doctor, and builds muscle, which is imperative in living a full life. The more we move, the more we accomplish, the better we think as more oxygen gets to the brain, and the more vibrant we become in our God-created, unique personality.

Sleep: Sleep is the key to a healthy life. Out of all three of the daily fundamentals, it is the heavy weight. Yes, we need to spend about one-third of our lives dormant. Don't you think God has a reason for that much rest, as we are His perfect design? Yes, eight hours is still the recommendation. We need to recover, refresh, repair and renew our mind, body and spirit with good sleep.

Today's Truth

As we go about our day, it is easier to keep our mind focused on the Lord if we choose one truth. Many times it can be as simple as, "Jesus loves me, this I know," a simple song from childhood. Or, it can be the verse we read today, or a Biblical truth, "God delights over me with singing." (Zephaniah 3:17), or "I walk in the Light as He is in the Light." (1 John 1:7)

Pick one, write it down and speak it over your life. It can be the same precept over and over, such as, "Be strong in the Lord and the Power of His Might" (Ephesians 6:10) or it can be a different one each day, "I can do all things through Christ Who strengthens me." (Philippians 4:13) Walk in His truth daily and see your mind be renewed, your purpose solidified and your tongue be tamed as "Life and death are in the power of the tongue." (Proverbs 18:21)

Evening Echoes

Gratitude

The more grateful we are, the more we grow in our vertical relationship with the Lord, and our horizontal relationship with others. Make gratitude a daily habit, morning and night. It will change your perspective on the world, others and yourself.

Goals for Tomorrow

The new day starts at sundown as it states in Genesis 1:5, "And God called the light Day, and the darkness He called Night. And the evening and the morning were the first day."

Plan the next day the night before so you can sleep better, feel more confident, and rest in the Lord. "All the days ordained for you were written down, even before one came to be." (Psalms 139: 16) In the morning, review the plan you made the night before so your day flows. Beware of "time-wasters" that keep you from accomplishing your goals. Also, be aware of perfectionism and negative thoughts that keep you frozen in fear and not hitting the target. Be faithful in journaling daily, and God will reveal your stumbling blocks. Make your goals specific and doable, as you want to set yourself up for success daily.

I Loved Others

God knew what He was doing when He said, "Love the Lord your God with all your heart, with all your soul and with all your might. Love your neighbor as yourself. On these two commandments rest the entire Law and Prophets." (Mark 12:31)

Pretty straight forward, isn't it? Love God and love your neighbors. Sometimes it is hard to love others, especially in our intimate relationships.

God asks of us, "Do not let the sun go down on your anger" (Ephesians 4:26) and to be a servant of all. "Anyone who wants to be first must be the very last, and the servant of all." (Mark 9:35)

Wow, tall orders. But, the Good News is we have the Holy Spirit living inside of us to help us love others. Just ask the Father to show you who to love today, how to love them, and the strength to accomplish it!

I Loved Myself

Yes, it is a given that we will love ourselves. "Love your neighbors as yourself." (Matthew 22:37-40) It's a requirement. Taking care of ourselves not only makes us feel and look better, but it tells our loving Heavenly Father that we appreciate the gift of life. It also helps us understand we were born for such a time as this as we have a purpose on this earth. We have a calling in life, a destiny to fulfill. We are fearfully and wonderfully made as we are unique. We are made in the image of God. "So God created mankind in His own image, in the image of God He created them; male and female He created them." (Genesis 1:27) Record how you loved yourself today.

Do Overs

Everyone falls short, makes mistakes and sins. We know that God forgives sin; all we have to do is ask and change our ways. "If we confess our sins, He is faithful and just to forgive us our sins, and to cleanse us from all unrighteousness." (1 John 1:9)

We all need do overs in life. Our goal as believers is to become more Christ-like every day. When we confess our sins, He forgives us. The Holy Spirit dwells within us to help us live as Jesus lived on this earth. Show yourself grace and write down what you wish you could do over from today.

Fundies (Fundamentals)

What choices did you make in the areas of eat, move and sleep today? Did you eat nourishing foods in a mindful manner? Did you move frequently and intentionally during the day? How many hours of sleep? Any naps today? If you can cement these three habits into your daily life, it will change your weeks, months and years. You will be amazed at what you can accomplish with your vibrant life.

A Loving Thought

God loves you as high as the heavens are above the earth. (Psalms 103:11) He also delights over you with singing, (Zephaniah 3:17) and He keeps you as the apple of His eye. (Psalms 17:8) If He adores you that much, of course He has loving thoughts toward you all day long. Ask Him and listen to what affirmation He wants to tell you before you fall asleep. Let your rest be sweet as your mind stays on Him. "You will keep him in perfect peace, whose mind is stayed on You, because he trusts in You." (Isaiah 26:3)

MONTHLY SUMMARIES

At the end of each month, you will ponder and meditate on the last 30 days and note the growth in your life. Celebrate the working of the Holy Spirit in your life and the lives of others as He who began a good work in you will be faithful to complete it. (Philippians 1:6)

Morning Meditations

Themes in Dreams

Did you have recurring themes in your dreams this month? The more you record your dreams, the easier it is to remember them. Look for patterns, themes and repetitive emotions. God can use our dreams to speak to us. Record, observe and learn from your dreams. They could be prophetic dreams of the future. If you cannot recall your dreams, ask the Father to help you remember. Do you dream in color? Pictures? What language? What age are you? Record the details of your dreams, immediately, upon awakening.

Patterns in Thoughts & Emotions

After recording your morning thoughts and feelings for 30 days, it will be easier to detect your emotional state and see patterns. Be honest with yourself and God. This is a private journal and a safe place to pen your raw thoughts and emotions. Check for hurts and ask God to heal you in those areas, if needed.

God's Messages

God loves to speak to us. He hides nuggets in His Word so we can search for them, and He rewards handsomely! Speak audibly to Him. Ask Him questions. Listen for the answers. He has loving surprises hid in His Word and your daily life. Start recognizing messages from God. Record it in the monthly summary.

Prayers Answered

This section is a faith-building one. Be sure to review your prayer requests from the last 30 days so you can celebrate God's answers. Some prayers are answered in a minute, and some we have to wait a lifetime, or longer, to know the answer. Either way, our God is so big, so strong and so mighty, there's nothing our God cannot do. (2 Corinthians 3:14)

Risks Conquered

What risks did you take this month? Which ones succeeded? Celebrate the small victories that lead to life changes. Journal how you felt after you took the risk. It will help your spiritual, physical, relational and entrepreneurial areas of your life. Live a bigger life!

Fundies (Fundamentals)

Did you eat sensibly, move frequently and sleep soundly this month? Look at the patterns. Celebrate the successes and plan on tiny changes for the next month. The key to implementing healthy habits into your life is the daily choices you make. We all feel better when we get enough sleep, ingest sound nutrition and destress with exercise.

Biggest Truths

Was there a specific truth that touched your heart this month? Did you record it multiple times? Note the change in your mindset. Do you have less anxiety? Clearer focus? More positive thoughts? Less negative ones? Have you learned to let go of trying to control life? Celebrate the wins in your journal!

Evening Summaries

Picture of God's Love for Me

Feel free to draw a picture, write a poem, or transcribe the words the Lord gave you. It may be impressions, feelings or intuitions. God uses all of our senses to speak to us. Be observant, and He will show you new and mighty things about Himself and His love for you. (Isaiah 43:19)

Gratitude Changes

What were you most thankful for this month? Did your attitude shift toward that person, place or thing? Gratitude absolutely changes the mindset and calms the soul. Note the changes and celebrate!

Goals Conquered

Recognize your goals accomplished this month. What did you do, and how did you do it? Small doable goals conquered daily lead to lifelong habits.

How I Loved Others

Record how you loved others throughout the month. Did you notice a pattern? Were some people harder to love than others? Are you changing your attitude toward the unlovable?

How I Loved Myself

Self-love is expected and commanded by God. How did you love yourself this month? List the ways. Continue to pursue self-care and take time for you. Grow in this area monthly. Love yourself well.

Grace for Do Overs

We all make mistakes daily. Always do your best and leave the rest to God. There are times when we need to ask God and others for forgiveness and to learn from our sins and errors. Showing grace and learning to laugh at yourself is important.

Thematic Loving Thoughts

Which thoughts were repeated throughout the month? What does your heart need to hear to heal? What truths soothe your soul? Continue to repeat it until it oozes from every pore of your being. Let it sink deep into your spirit.

Enjoy the process as the Holy Spirit infuses hope and inspires action in your life. "Beloved, I pray that you may prosper in all things and be in good health, just as your soul prospers." (3 John 2)

The Lord is close to the brokenhearted and
saves those who are crushed in spirit.
Psalm 34:18

Delight yourself in the Lord, and He will
give you the desires of your heart.
Psalm 37:4

For You created my inmost being; You knit
me together in my mother's womb.
Psalm 139:13

Month

1

Morning Meditations

Date _____   Psalms _____

Dreams

Thoughts and Emotions

Gratitude

Psalms Messages

Prayers

Risk Today

Fundies

Today's Truth

Gratitude

Goals for Tomorrow

I Loved Others

I Loved Myself

Do Overs from Today

Fundies

A Loving Thought

Morning Meditations

Date   Psalms

Dreams

Thoughts and Emotions

Gratitude

Psalms Messages

Prayers

Risk Today

Fundies

Today's Truth

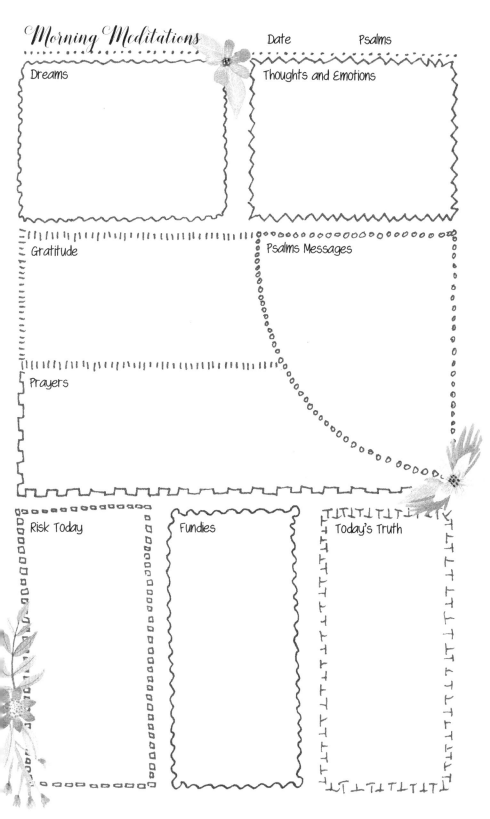

Gratitude

Goals for Tomorrow

I Loved Others

I Loved Myself

Do Overs from Today

Fundies

A Loving Thought

Morning Meditations

Date   Psalms

Dreams

Thoughts and Emotions

Gratitude

Psalms Messages

Prayers

Risk Today

Fundies

Today's Truth

Evening Echoes

Gratitude

Goals for Tomorrow

I Loved Others

I Loved Myself

Do Overs from Today

Fundies

A Loving Thought

Morning Meditations

Date _____ Psalms _____

Dreams

Thoughts and Emotions

Gratitude

Psalms Messages

Prayers

Risk Today

Fundies

Today's Truth

Gratitude

Goals for Tomorrow

I Loved Others

I Loved Myself

Do Overs from Today

Fundies

A Loving Thought

Morning Meditations

Date   Psalms

Dreams

Thoughts and Emotions

Gratitude

Psalms Messages

Prayers

Risk Today

Fundies

Today's Truth

Gratitude

Goals for Tomorrow

I Loved Others

I Loved Myself

Do Overs from Today

Fundies

A Loving Thought

Morning Meditations

Date   Psalms

Dreams

Thoughts and Emotions

Gratitude

Psalms Messages

Prayers

Risk Today

Fundies

Today's Truth

Evening Echoes

Gratitude

Goals for Tomorrow

I Loved Others

I Loved Myself

Do Overs from Today

Fundies

A Loving Thought

Morning Meditations

Date   Psalms

Dreams

Thoughts and Emotions

Gratitude

Psalms Messages

Prayers

Risk Today

Fundies

Today's Truth

Evening Echoes

Gratitude

Goals for Tomorrow

I Loved Others

I Loved Myself

Do Overs from Today

Fundies

A Loving Thought

Morning Meditations

Date .... Psalms ....

Dreams

Thoughts and Emotions

Gratitude

Psalms Messages

Prayers

Risk Today

Fundies

Today's Truth

Gratitude

Goals for Tomorrow

I Loved Others

I Loved Myself

Do Overs from Today

Fundies

A Loving Thought

Morning Meditations

Date   Psalms

Dreams

Thoughts and Emotions

Gratitude

Psalms Messages

Prayers

Risk Today

Fundies

Today's Truth

Evening Echoes

Gratitude

Goals for Tomorrow

I Loved Others

I Loved Myself

Do Overs from Today

Fundies

A Loving Thought

Morning Meditations

Date   Psalms

Dreams

Thoughts and Emotions

Gratitude

Psalms Messages

Prayers

Risk Today

Fundies

Today's Truth

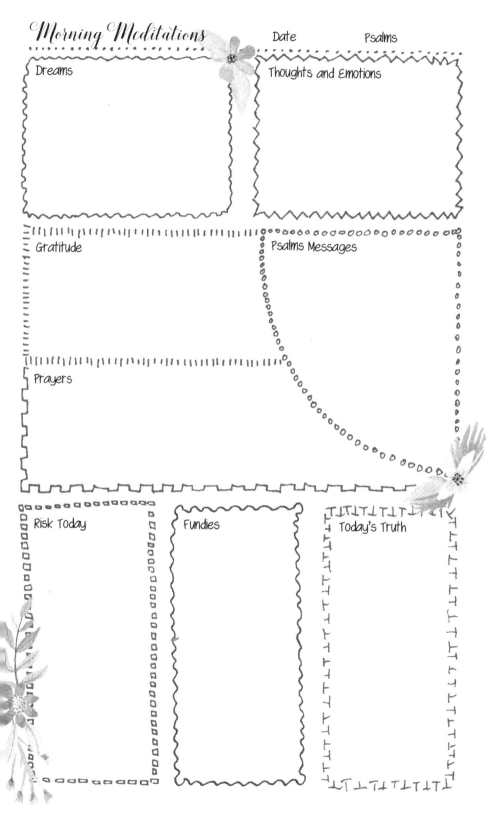

Evening Echoes

Gratitude

Goals for Tomorrow

I Loved Others

I Loved Myself

Do Overs from Today

Fundies

A Loving Thought

Morning Meditations

Date   Psalms

Dreams

Thoughts and Emotions

Gratitude

Psalms Messages

Prayers

Risk Today

Fundies

Today's Truth

Gratitude

Goals for Tomorrow

I Loved Others

I Loved Myself

Do Overs from Today

Fundies

A Loving Thought

Morning Meditations

Date _____   Psalms _____

Dreams

Thoughts and Emotions

Gratitude

Psalms Messages

Prayers

Risk Today

Fundies

Today's Truth

Evening Echoes

Gratitude

Goals for Tomorrow

I Loved Others

I Loved Myself

Do Overs from Today

Fundies

A Loving Thought

Morning Meditations

Date   Psalms

Dreams

Thoughts and Emotions

Gratitude

Psalms Messages

Prayers

Risk Today

Fundies

Today's Truth

Evening Echoes

Gratitude

Goals for Tomorrow

I Loved Others

I Loved Myself

Do Overs from Today

Fundies

A Loving Thought

Morning Meditations

Date   Psalms

Dreams

Thoughts and Emotions

Gratitude

Psalms Messages

Prayers

Risk Today

Fundies

Today's Truth

Evening Echoes

Gratitude

Goals for Tomorrow

I Loved Others

I Loved Myself

Do Overs from Today

Fundies

A Loving Thought

Morning Meditations

Date _____   Psalms _____

Dreams

Thoughts and Emotions

Gratitude

Psalms Messages

Prayers

Risk Today

Fundies

Today's Truth

Gratitude

Goals for Tomorrow

I Loved Others

I Loved Myself

Do Overs from Today

Fundies

A Loving Thought

Morning Meditations

Date   Psalms

Dreams

Thoughts and Emotions

Gratitude

Psalms Messages

Prayers

Risk Today

Fundies

Today's Truth

Evening Echoes

Gratitude

Goals for Tomorrow

I Loved Others

I Loved Myself

Do Overs from Today

Fundies

A Loving Thought

Morning Meditations

Date   Psalms

Dreams

Thoughts and Emotions

Gratitude

Psalms Messages

Prayers

Risk Today

Fundies

Today's Truth

Gratitude

Goals for Tomorrow

I Loved Others

I Loved Myself

Do Overs from Today

Fundies

A Loving Thought

Morning Meditations

Date   Psalms

Dreams

Thoughts and Emotions

Gratitude

Psalms Messages

Prayers

Risk Today

Fundies

Today's Truth

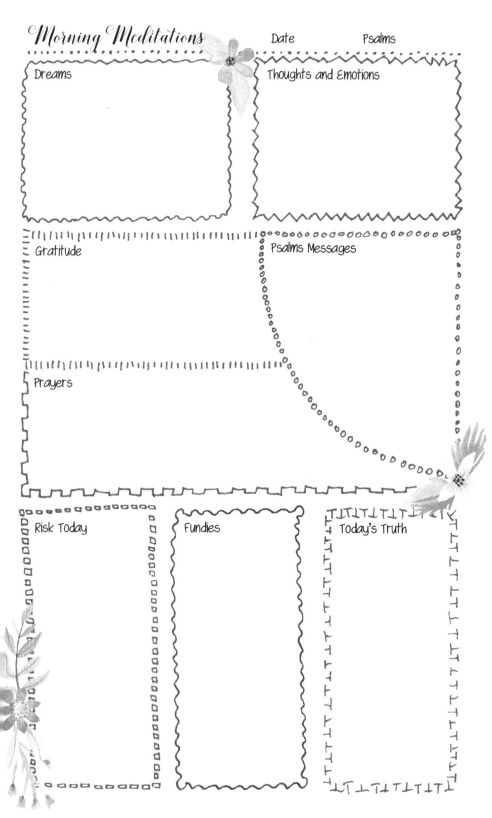

Evening Echoes

Gratitude

Goals for Tomorrow

I Loved Others

I Loved Myself

Do Overs from Today

Fundies

A Loving Thought

Morning Meditations

Date   Psalms

Dreams

Thoughts and Emotions

Gratitude

Psalms Messages

Prayers

Risk Today

Fundies

Today's Truth

Gratitude

Goals for Tomorrow

I Loved Others

I Loved Myself

Do Overs from Today

Fundies

A Loving Thought

Morning Meditations

Date   Psalms

Dreams

Thoughts and Emotions

Gratitude

Psalms Messages

Prayers

Risk Today

Fundies

Today's Truth

Gratitude

Goals for Tomorrow

I Loved Others

I Loved Myself

Do Overs from Today

Fundies

A Loving Thought

Morning Meditations

Date   Psalms

Dreams

Thoughts and Emotions

Gratitude

Psalms Messages

Prayers

Risk Today

Fundies

Today's Truth

Gratitude

Goals for Tomorrow

I Loved Others

I Loved Myself

Do Overs from Today

Fundies

A Loving Thought

Morning Meditations

Date   Psalms

Dreams

Thoughts and Emotions

Gratitude

Psalms Messages

Prayers

Risk Today

Fundies

Today's Truth

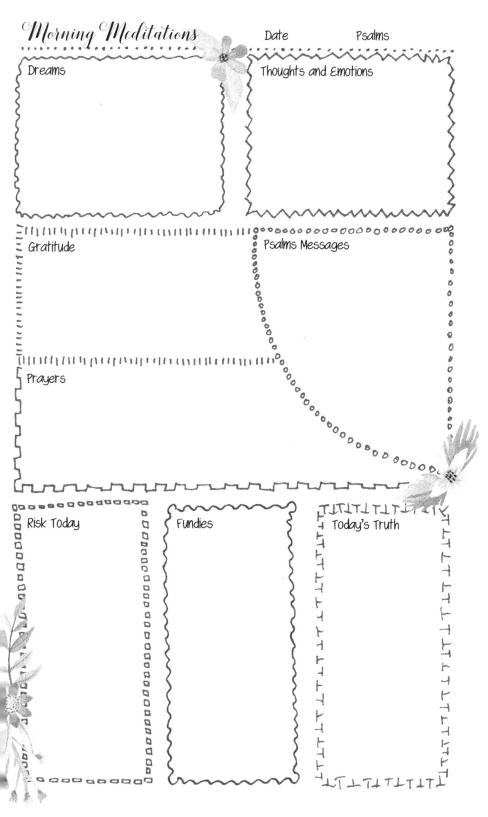

Gratitude

Goals for Tomorrow

I Loved Others

I Loved Myself

Do Overs from Today

Fundies

A Loving Thought

Morning Meditations

Date   Psalms

Dreams

Thoughts and Emotions

Gratitude

Psalms Messages

Prayers

Risk Today

Fundies

Today's Truth

Gratitude

Goals for Tomorrow

I Loved Others

I Loved Myself

Do Overs from Today

Fundies

A Loving Thought

Morning Meditations

Date .... Psalms ....

Dreams

Thoughts and Emotions

Gratitude

Psalms Messages

Prayers

Risk Today

Fundies

Today's Truth

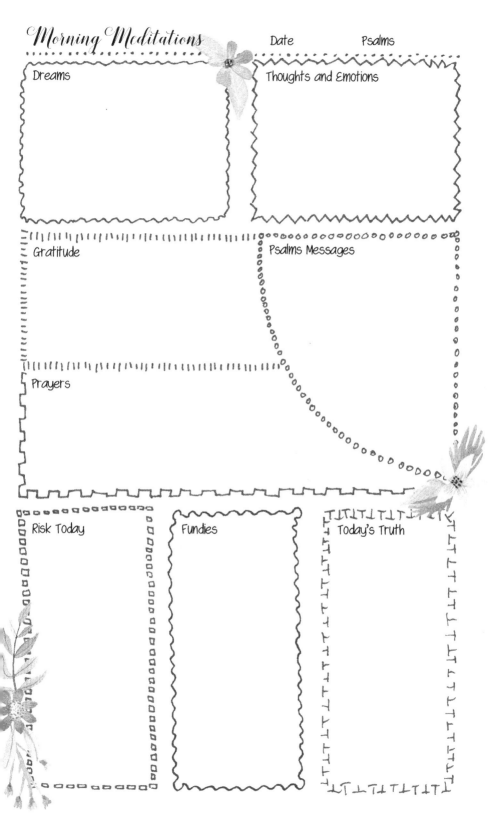

Gratitude

Goals for Tomorrow

I Loved Others

I Loved Myself

Do Overs from Today

Fundies

A Loving Thought

Morning Meditations

Date   Psalms

Dreams

Thoughts and Emotions

Gratitude

Psalms Messages

Prayers

Risk Today

Fundies

Today's Truth

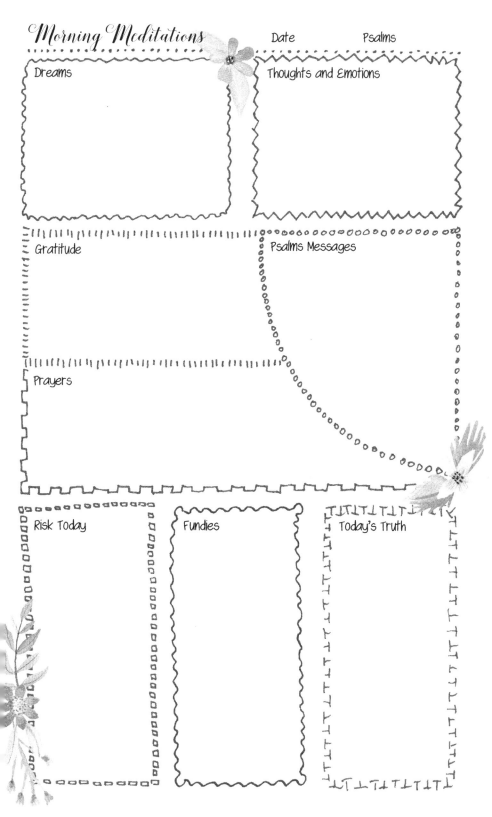

Gratitude

Goals for Tomorrow

I Loved Others

I Loved Myself

Do Overs from Today

Fundies

A Loving Thought

Morning Meditations

Date   Psalms

Dreams

Thoughts and Emotions

Gratitude

Psalms Messages

Prayers

Risk Today

Fundies

Today's Truth

Gratitude

Goals for Tomorrow

I Loved Others

I Loved Myself

Do Overs from Today

Fundies

A Loving Thought

Morning Meditations

Date   Psalms

Dreams

Thoughts and Emotions

Gratitude

Psalms Messages

Prayers

Risk Today

Fundies

Today's Truth

Gratitude

Goals for Tomorrow

I Loved Others

I Loved Myself

Do Overs from Today

Fundies

A Loving Thought

Morning Meditations

Date   Psalms

Dreams

Thoughts and Emotions

Gratitude

Psalms Messages

Prayers

Risk Today

Fundies

Today's Truth

Gratitude

Goals for Tomorrow

I Loved Others

I Loved Myself

Do Overs from Today

Fundies

A Loving Thought

Morning Meditations

Date   Psalms

Dreams

Thoughts and Emotions

Gratitude

Psalms Messages

Prayers

Risk Today

Fundies

Today's Truth

Gratitude

Goals for Tomorrow

I Loved Others

I Loved Myself

Do Overs from Today

Fundies

A Loving Thought

Morning Meditations

Date   Psalms

Dreams

Thoughts and Emotions

Gratitude

Psalms Messages

Prayers

Risk Today

Fundies

Today's Truth

Evening Echoes

Gratitude

Goals for Tomorrow

I Loved Others

I Loved Myself

Do Overs from Today

Fundies

A Loving Thought

Create in me a pure heart, O God,
and renew a steadfast spirit within me.
Psalm 51:10

Behold, children are a gift of the Lord, The fruit of
the womb is a reward.
Psalm 127:3

Cast your cares on the Lord and He will sustain you.
Psalm 55:22

Month
1
Summary

Morning Monthly Summary

Date

Psalms Read

Themes in Dreams

Patterns in Thoughts & Emotions

God's Messages

Prayers Answered

Risks Conquered

Fundies

Biggest Truths

Evening Monthly Summary

Picture of God's Love for Me

Gratitude Changes

Goals Conquered

How I Loved Others

How I Loved Myself

Grace for Do Overs

Thematic Loving Thoughts

Your word is a lamp for my feet, a light on my path.
Psalm 119:105

When anxiety was great within me,
Your consolation brought me joy.
Psalm 94:19

I sought the Lord, and He answered me;
He delivered me from all my fears.
Psalm 34:4

Month

2

Morning Meditations

Date   Psalms

Dreams

Thoughts and Emotions

Gratitude

Psalms Messages

Prayers

Risk Today

Fundies

Today's Truth

Gratitude

Goals for Tomorrow

I Loved Others

I Loved Myself

Do Overs from Today

Fundies

A Loving Thought

Morning Meditations

Date   Psalms

Dreams

Thoughts and Emotions

Gratitude

Psalms Messages

Prayers

Risk Today

Fundies

Today's Truth

Gratitude

Goals for Tomorrow

I Loved Others

I Loved Myself

Do Overs from Today

Fundies

A Loving Thought

Morning Meditations

Date   Psalms

Dreams

Thoughts and Emotions

Gratitude

Psalms Messages

Prayers

Risk Today

Fundies

Today's Truth

Gratitude

Goals for Tomorrow

I Loved Others

I Loved Myself

Do Overs from Today

Fundies

A Loving Thought

Morning Meditations

Date

Psalms

Dreams

Thoughts and Emotions

Gratitude

Psalms Messages

Prayers

Risk Today

Fundies

Today's Truth

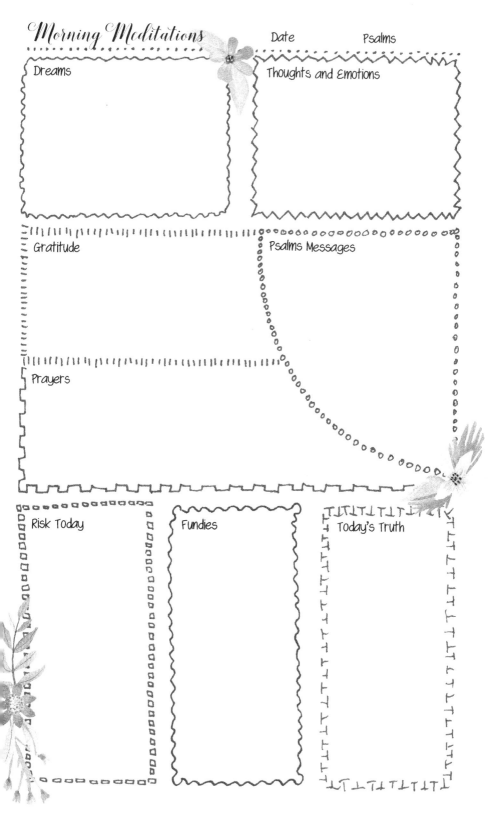

Evening Echoes

Gratitude

Goals for Tomorrow

I Loved Others

I Loved Myself

Do Overs from Today

Fundies

A Loving Thought

Morning Meditations

Date   Psalms

Dreams

Thoughts and Emotions

Gratitude

Psalms Messages

Prayers

Risk Today

Fundies

Today's Truth

Evening Echoes

Gratitude

Goals for Tomorrow

I Loved Others

I Loved Myself

Do Overs from Today

Fundies

A Loving Thought

Morning Meditations

Date   Psalms

Dreams

Thoughts and Emotions

Gratitude

Psalms Messages

Prayers

Risk Today

Fundies

Today's Truth

Gratitude

Goals for Tomorrow

I Loved Others

I Loved Myself

Do Overs from Today

Fundies

A Loving Thought

Morning Meditations

Date   Psalms

Dreams

Thoughts and Emotions

Gratitude

Psalms Messages

Prayers

Risk Today

Fundies

Today's Truth

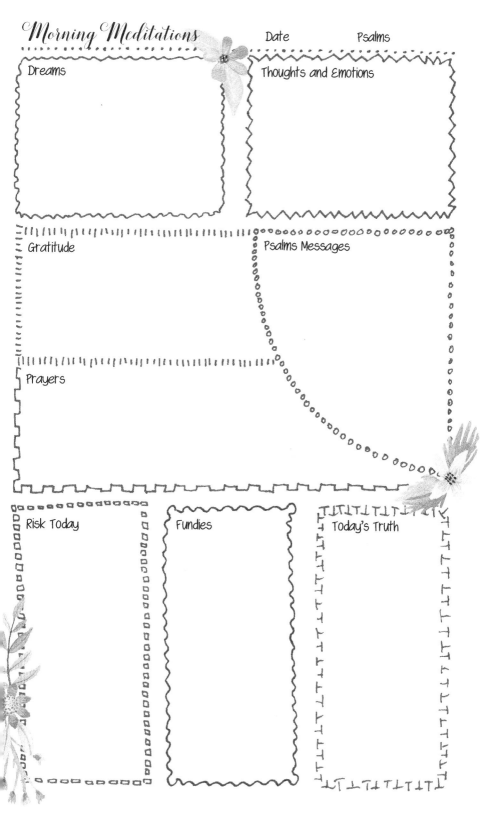

Gratitude

Goals for Tomorrow

I Loved Others

I Loved Myself

Do Overs from Today

Fundies

A Loving Thought

Morning Meditations

Date _____   Psalms _____

Dreams

Thoughts and Emotions

Gratitude

Psalms Messages

Prayers

Risk Today

Fundies

Today's Truth

Evening Echoes

Gratitude

Goals for Tomorrow

I Loved Others

I Loved Myself

Do Overs from Today

Fundies

A Loving Thought

Morning Meditations

Date   Psalms

Dreams

Thoughts and Emotions

Gratitude

Psalms Messages

Prayers

Risk Today

Fundies

Today's Truth

Gratitude

Goals for Tomorrow

I Loved Others

I Loved Myself

Do Overs from Today

Fundies

A Loving Thought

Morning Meditations

Date   Psalms

Dreams

Thoughts and Emotions

Gratitude

Psalms Messages

Prayers

Risk Today

Fundies

Today's Truth

Evening Echoes

Gratitude

Goals for Tomorrow

I Loved Others

I Loved Myself

Do Overs from Today

Fundies

A Loving Thought

Morning Meditations

Date   Psalms

Dreams

Thoughts and Emotions

Gratitude

Psalms Messages

Prayers

Risk Today

Fundies

Today's Truth

Evening Echoes

Gratitude

Goals for Tomorrow

I Loved Others

I Loved Myself

Do Overs from Today

Fundies

A Loving Thought

Morning Meditations

Date   Psalms

Dreams

Thoughts and Emotions

Gratitude

Psalms Messages

Prayers

Risk Today

Fundies

Today's Truth

Gratitude

Goals for Tomorrow

I Loved Others

I Loved Myself

Do Overs from Today

Fundies

A Loving Thought

Morning Meditations

Date   Psalms

Dreams

Thoughts and Emotions

Gratitude

Psalms Messages

Prayers

Risk Today

Fundies

Today's Truth

Gratitude

Goals for Tomorrow

I Loved Others

I Loved Myself

Do Overs from Today

Fundies

A Loving Thought

Morning Meditations

Date   Psalms

Dreams

Thoughts and Emotions

Gratitude

Psalms Messages

Prayers

Risk Today

Fundies

Today's Truth

Gratitude

Goals for Tomorrow

I Loved Others

I Loved Myself

Do Overs from Today

Fundies

A Loving Thought

Morning Meditations

Date   Psalms

Dreams

Thoughts and Emotions

Gratitude

Psalms Messages

Prayers

Risk Today

Fundies

Today's Truth

Gratitude

Goals for Tomorrow

I Loved Others

I Loved Myself

Do Overs from Today

Fundies

A Loving Thought

Morning Meditations

Date _____ Psalms _____

Dreams

Thoughts and Emotions

Gratitude

Psalms Messages

Prayers

Risk Today

Fundies

Today's Truth

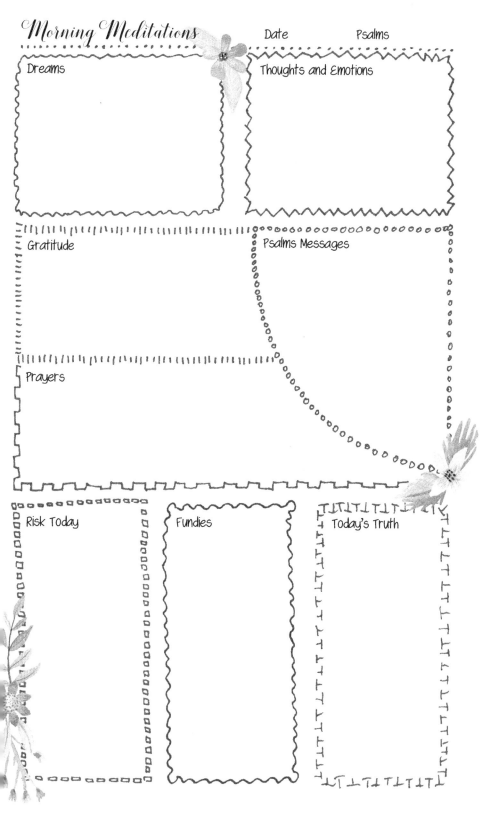

Gratitude

Goals for Tomorrow

I Loved Others

I Loved Myself

Do Overs from Today

Fundies

A Loving Thought

Morning Meditations

Date _____ Psalms _____

Dreams

Thoughts and Emotions

Gratitude

Psalms Messages

Prayers

Risk Today

Fundies

Today's Truth

Gratitude

Goals for Tomorrow

I Loved Others

I Loved Myself

Do Overs from Today

Fundies

A Loving Thought

Morning Meditations

Date   Psalms

Dreams

Thoughts and Emotions

Gratitude

Psalms Messages

Prayers

Risk Today

Fundies

Today's Truth

Evening Echoes

Gratitude

Goals for Tomorrow

I Loved Others

I Loved Myself

Do Overs from Today

Fundies

A Loving Thought

Morning Meditations

Date   Psalms

Dreams

Thoughts and Emotions

Gratitude

Psalms Messages

Prayers

Risk Today

Fundies

Today's Truth

Gratitude

Goals for Tomorrow

I Loved Others

I Loved Myself

Do Overs from Today

Fundies

A Loving Thought

Morning Meditations

Date   Psalms

Dreams

Thoughts and Emotions

Gratitude

Psalms Messages

Prayers

Risk Today

Fundies

Today's Truth

Gratitude

Goals for Tomorrow

I Loved Others

I Loved Myself

Do Overs from Today

Fundies

A Loving Thought

Morning Meditations

Date   Psalms

Dreams

Thoughts and Emotions

Gratitude

Psalms Messages

Prayers

Risk Today

Fundies

Today's Truth

Gratitude

Goals for Tomorrow

I Loved Others

I Loved Myself

Do Overs from Today

Fundies

A Loving Thought

Morning Meditations

Date   Psalms

Dreams

Thoughts and Emotions

Gratitude

Psalms Messages

Prayers

Risk Today

Fundies

Today's Truth

Gratitude

Goals for Tomorrow

I Loved Others

I Loved Myself

Do Overs from Today

Fundies

A Loving Thought

Morning Meditations

Date   Psalms

Dreams

Thoughts and Emotions

Gratitude

Psalms Messages

Prayers

Risk Today

Fundies

Today's Truth

Gratitude

Goals for Tomorrow

I Loved Others

I Loved Myself

Do Overs from Today

Fundies

A Loving Thought

Morning Meditations

Date　　　　　Psalms

Dreams

Thoughts and Emotions

Gratitude

Psalms Messages

Prayers

Risk Today

Fundies

Today's Truth

Evening Echoes

Gratitude

Goals for Tomorrow

I Loved Others

I Loved Myself

Do Overs from Today

Fundies

A Loving Thought

Morning Meditations

Date   Psalms

Dreams

Thoughts and Emotions

Gratitude

Psalms Messages

Prayers

Risk Today

Fundies

Today's Truth

Evening Echoes

Gratitude

Goals for Tomorrow

I Loved Others

I Loved Myself

Do Overs from Today

Fundies

A Loving Thought

Morning Meditations

Date   Psalms

Dreams

Thoughts and Emotions

Gratitude

Psalms Messages

Prayers

Risk Today

Fundies

Today's Truth

Gratitude

Goals for Tomorrow

I Loved Others

I Loved Myself

Do Overs from Today

Fundies

A Loving Thought

Morning Meditations

Date　　　　Psalms

Dreams

Thoughts and Emotions

Gratitude

Psalms Messages

Prayers

Risk Today

Fundies

Today's Truth

Gratitude

Goals for Tomorrow

I Loved Others

I Loved Myself

Do Overs from Today

Fundies

A Loving Thought

Morning Meditations

Date   Psalms

Dreams

Thoughts and Emotions

Gratitude

Psalms Messages

Prayers

Risk Today

Fundies

Today's Truth

Gratitude

Goals for Tomorrow

I Loved Others

I Loved Myself

Do Overs from Today

Fundies

A Loving Thought

Morning Meditations

Date .... Psalms ....

Dreams

Thoughts and Emotions

Gratitude

Psalms Messages

Prayers

Risk Today

Fundies

Today's Truth

Gratitude

Goals for Tomorrow

I Loved Others

I Loved Myself

Do Overs from Today

Fundies

A Loving Thought

Morning Meditations

Date .... Psalms

Dreams

Thoughts and Emotions

Gratitude

Psalms Messages

Prayers

Risk Today

Fundies

Today's Truth

Gratitude

Goals for Tomorrow

I Loved Others

I Loved Myself

Do Overs from Today

Fundies

A Loving Thought

He is like a tree
planted by streams of water
that yields its fruit in its season,
and its leaf does not wither.
In all that he does, he prospers.
Psalm 1:3

The Lord is close to the brokenhearted and
saves those who are crushed in spirit.
Psalm 34:18

Wait for the Lord; be strong and take heart
and wait for the Lord.
Psalm 27:14

Month
2
Summary

Morning Monthly Summary

Date

Psalms Read

Themes in Dreams

Patterns in Thoughts & Emotions

God's Messages

Prayers Answered

Risks Conquered

Fundies

Biggest Truths

Evening Monthly Summary

Picture of God's Love for Me

Gratitude Changes

Goals Conquered

How I Loved Others

How I Loved Myself

Grace for Do Overs

Thematic Loving Thoughts

O Lord, my heart is not lifted up;
my eyes are not raised too high;
I do not occupy myself with things
too great and too marvelous for me.
But I have calmed and quieted my soul,
like a weaned child with its mother;
like a weaned child is my soul within me.
Psalm 131:1-2

You keep track of all my sorrows. You have
collected all my tears in your bottle. You
have recorded each one in your book.
Psalm 56:8

I will praise the Lord, who counsels me; even
at night my heart instructs me.
Psalm 16:7

Month

3

Morning Meditations

Date   Psalms

Dreams

Thoughts and Emotions

Gratitude

Psalms Messages

Prayers

Risk Today

Fundies

Today's Truth

Gratitude

Goals for Tomorrow

I Loved Others

I Loved Myself

Do Overs from Today

Fundies

A Loving Thought

Morning Meditations

Date   Psalms

Dreams

Thoughts and Emotions

Gratitude

Psalms Messages

Prayers

Risk Today

Fundies

Today's Truth

Gratitude

Goals for Tomorrow

I Loved Others

I Loved Myself

Do Overs from Today

Fundies

A Loving Thought

Morning Meditations

Date   Psalms

Dreams

Thoughts and Emotions

Gratitude

Psalms Messages

Prayers

Risk Today

Fundies

Today's Truth

Gratitude

Goals for Tomorrow

I Loved Others

I Loved Myself

Do Overs from Today

Fundies

A Loving Thought

Morning Meditations

Date   Psalms

Dreams

Thoughts and Emotions

Gratitude

Psalms Messages

Prayers

Risk Today

Fundies

Today's Truth

Gratitude

Goals for Tomorrow

I Loved Others

I Loved Myself

Do Overs from Today

Fundies

A Loving Thought

Morning Meditations

Date   Psalms

Dreams

Thoughts and Emotions

Gratitude

Psalms Messages

Prayers

Risk Today

Fundies

Today's Truth

Gratitude

Goals for Tomorrow

I Loved Others

I Loved Myself

Do Overs from Today

Fundies

A Loving Thought

Morning Meditations

Date   Psalms

Dreams

Thoughts and Emotions

Gratitude

Psalms Messages

Prayers

Risk Today

Fundies

Today's Truth

Evening Echoes

Gratitude

Goals for Tomorrow

I Loved Others

I Loved Myself

Do Overs from Today

Fundies

A Loving Thought

Morning Meditations

Date   Psalms

Dreams

Thoughts and Emotions

Gratitude

Psalms Messages

Prayers

Risk Today

Fundies

Today's Truth

Gratitude

Goals for Tomorrow

I Loved Others

I Loved Myself

Do Overs from Today

Fundies

A Loving Thought

Morning Meditations

Date   Psalms

Dreams

Thoughts and Emotions

Gratitude

Psalms Messages

Prayers

Risk Today

Fundies

Today's Truth

Gratitude

Goals for Tomorrow

I Loved Others

I Loved Myself

Do Overs from Today

Fundies

A Loving Thought

Morning Meditations

Date   Psalms

Dreams

Thoughts and Emotions

Gratitude

Psalms Messages

Prayers

Risk Today

Fundies

Today's Truth

Evening Echoes

Gratitude

Goals for Tomorrow

I Loved Others

I Loved Myself

Do Overs from Today

Fundies

A Loving Thought

Morning Meditations

Date   Psalms

Dreams

Thoughts and Emotions

Gratitude

Psalms Messages

Prayers

Risk Today

Fundies

Today's Truth

Gratitude

Goals for Tomorrow

I Loved Others

I Loved Myself

Do Overs from Today

Fundies

A Loving Thought

Morning Meditations

Date   Psalms

Dreams

Thoughts and Emotions

Gratitude

Psalms Messages

Prayers

Risk Today

Fundies

Today's Truth

Evening Echoes

Gratitude

Goals for Tomorrow

I Loved Others

I Loved Myself

Do Overs from Today

Fundies

A Loving Thought

Morning Meditations

Date   Psalms

Dreams

Thoughts and Emotions

Gratitude

Psalms Messages

Prayers

Risk Today

Fundies

Today's Truth

Gratitude

Goals for Tomorrow

I Loved Others

I Loved Myself

Do Overs from Today

Fundies

A Loving Thought

Morning Meditations

Date _____ Psalms _____

Dreams

Thoughts and Emotions

Gratitude

Psalms Messages

Prayers

Risk Today

Fundies

Today's Truth

Evening Echoes

Gratitude

Goals for Tomorrow

I Loved Others

I Loved Myself

Do Overs from Today

Fundies

A Loving Thought

Morning Meditations

Date   Psalms

Dreams

Thoughts and Emotions

Gratitude

Psalms Messages

Prayers

Risk Today

Fundies

Today's Truth

Gratitude

Goals for Tomorrow

I Loved Others

I Loved Myself

Do Overs from Today

Fundies

A Loving Thought

Morning Meditations

Date   Psalms

Dreams

Thoughts and Emotions

Gratitude

Psalms Messages

Prayers

Risk Today

Fundies

Today's Truth

Evening Echoes

Gratitude

Goals for Tomorrow

I Loved Others

I Loved Myself

Do Overs from Today

Fundies

A Loving Thought

Morning Meditations

Date   Psalms

Dreams

Thoughts and Emotions

Gratitude

Psalms Messages

Prayers

Risk Today

Fundies

Today's Truth

Gratitude

Goals for Tomorrow

I Loved Others

I Loved Myself

Do Overs from Today

Fundies

A Loving Thought

Morning Meditations

Date   Psalms

Dreams

Thoughts and Emotions

Gratitude

Psalms Messages

Prayers

Risk Today

Fundies

Today's Truth

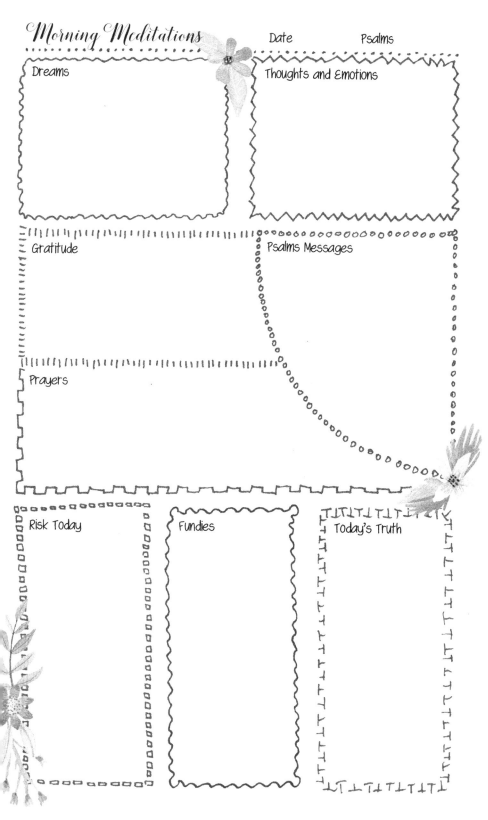

Gratitude

Goals for Tomorrow

I Loved Others

I Loved Myself

Do Overs from Today

Fundies

A Loving Thought

Morning Meditations

Date   Psalms

Dreams

Thoughts and Emotions

Gratitude

Psalms Messages

Prayers

Risk Today

Fundies

Today's Truth

Evening Echoes

Gratitude

Goals for Tomorrow

I Loved Others

I Loved Myself

Do Overs from Today

Fundies

A Loving Thought

Morning Meditations

Date   Psalms

Dreams

Thoughts and Emotions

Gratitude

Psalms Messages

Prayers

Risk Today

Fundies

Today's Truth

Evening Echoes

Gratitude

Goals for Tomorrow

I Loved Others

I Loved Myself

Do Overs from Today

Fundies

A Loving Thought

Morning Meditations

Date   Psalms

Dreams

Thoughts and Emotions

Gratitude

Psalms Messages

Prayers

Risk Today

Fundies

Today's Truth

Gratitude

Goals for Tomorrow

I Loved Others

I Loved Myself

Do Overs from Today

Fundies

A Loving Thought

Morning Meditations

Date   Psalms

Dreams

Thoughts and Emotions

Gratitude

Psalms Messages

Prayers

Risk Today

Fundies

Today's Truth

Gratitude

Goals for Tomorrow

I Loved Others

I Loved Myself

Do Overs from Today

Fundies

A Loving Thought

Morning Meditations

Date   Psalms

Dreams

Thoughts and Emotions

Gratitude

Psalms Messages

Prayers

Risk Today

Fundies

Today's Truth

Evening Echoes

Gratitude

Goals for Tomorrow

I Loved Others

I Loved Myself

Do Overs from Today

Fundies

A Loving Thought

Morning Meditations

Date   Psalms

Dreams

Thoughts and Emotions

Gratitude

Psalms Messages

Prayers

Risk Today

Fundies

Today's Truth

Gratitude

Goals for Tomorrow

I Loved Others

I Loved Myself

Do Overs from Today

Fundies

A Loving Thought

Morning Meditations

Date   Psalms

Dreams

Thoughts and Emotions

Gratitude

Psalms Messages

Prayers

Risk Today

Fundies

Today's Truth

Gratitude

Goals for Tomorrow

I Loved Others

I Loved Myself

Do Overs from Today

Fundies

A Loving Thought

Morning Meditations

Date   Psalms

Dreams

Thoughts and Emotions

Gratitude

Psalms Messages

Prayers

Risk Today

Fundies

Today's Truth

Evening Echoes

Gratitude

Goals for Tomorrow

I Loved Others

I Loved Myself

Do Overs from Today

Fundies

A Loving Thought

Morning Meditations

Date   Psalms

Dreams

Thoughts and Emotions

Gratitude

Psalms Messages

Prayers

Risk Today

Fundies

Today's Truth

Gratitude

Goals for Tomorrow

I Loved Others

I Loved Myself

Do Overs from Today

Fundies

A Loving Thought

Morning Meditations

Date   Psalms

Dreams

Thoughts and Emotions

Gratitude

Psalms Messages

Prayers

Risk Today

Fundies

Today's Truth

Gratitude

Goals for Tomorrow

I Loved Others

I Loved Myself

Do Overs from Today

Fundies

A Loving Thought

Morning Meditations

Date   Psalms

Dreams

Thoughts and Emotions

Gratitude

Psalms Messages

Prayers

Risk Today

Fundies

Today's Truth

Gratitude

Goals for Tomorrow

I Loved Others

I Loved Myself

Do Overs from Today

Fundies

A Loving Thought

Morning Meditations

Date   Psalms

Dreams

Thoughts and Emotions

Gratitude

Psalms Messages

Prayers

Risk Today

Fundies

Today's Truth

Gratitude

Goals for Tomorrow

I Loved Others

I Loved Myself

Do Overs from Today

Fundies

A Loving Thought

Morning Meditations

Date   Psalms

Dreams

Thoughts and Emotions

Gratitude

Psalms Messages

Prayers

Risk Today

Fundies

Today's Truth

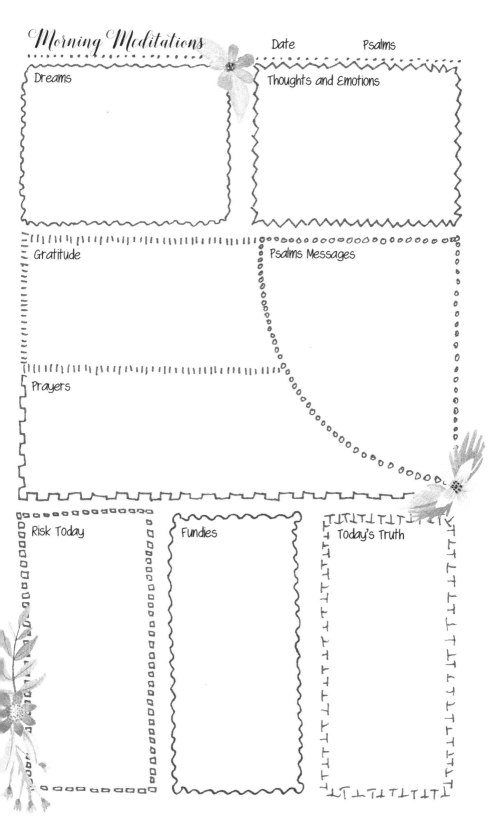

Evening Echoes

Gratitude

Goals for Tomorrow

I Loved Others

I Loved Myself

Do Overs from Today

Fundies

A Loving Thought

May God be gracious to us and bless us and
make His face shine on us.
Psalm 67:1

Let the words of my mouth and the medita-
tion of my heart be acceptable in Your sight,
O Lord, my rock and my redeemer.
Psalm 19:14

When anxiety was great within me, Your
consolation brought me joy.
Psalm 94:19

Month 3 Summary

Morning Monthly Summary

Date

Psalms Read

Themes in Dreams

Patterns in Thoughts & Emotions

God's Messages

Prayers Answered

Risks Conquered

Fundies

Biggest Truths

Evening Monthly Summary

Picture of God's Love for Me

Gratitude Changes

Goals Conquered

How I Loved Others

How I Loved Myself

Grace for Do Overs

Thematic Loving Thoughts

ABOUT THE AUTHOR

Janita Pavelka is a woman who loves to praise the Lord the way King David did in the Psalms. For many years, God had her "camped" in that book of the Bible and this journal is the result of her extensive study. Janita meditated on each chapter and verse as part of her daily devotions. She still finds incredible inspiration just like King David must have experienced as he penned the Psalms. She is a musician who praises through her hands and her instruments. What's more, she's become a writer who praises through her pen!

Janita loves to glorify God, and help people as she finds deep joy in the creation of life-giving projects. Pavelka writes in her journal nearly every day and has dedicated herself to the process. She admits she is a dreamer, but she's extremely action-oriented. Her motto in life is to "infuse hope and inspire action." She personifies it in herself and encourages it in others.

Janita has degrees in social work, psychology and education which all make her highly relational. Pavelka is a popular educator, workshop presenter, speaker, and author. When she isn't knee-deep in creative projects, Janita loves to spend time with her husband and family on their Old MacDonald's farm in south-central Nebraska.

☐ Psalm 1:1–3 How blessed is the woman who does not walk in the counsel of the wicked, Nor stand in the path of sinners, Nor sit in the seat of scoffers! But her delight is in the law of the LORD, And in His law she meditates day and night. She will be like a tree firmly planted by streams of water, which yields its fruit in its season And its leaf does not wither; And in whatever she does, she prospers.

☐ Psalm 2:1-4 The kings of the earth take their stand And the rulers take counsel together Against the LORD and against His Anointed, saying, "Let us tear their fetters apart And cast away their cords from us!" He who sits in the heavens laughs, The Lord scoffs at them.

☐ Psalm 24:3-6 Who may ascend into the hill of the LORD? And who may stand in His holy place? She who has clean hands and a pure heart, who has not lifted up her soul to falsehood And has not sworn deceitfully. She shall receive a blessing from the LORD And righteousness from the God of his salvation. This is the generation of those who seek Him, Who seek Your face.

☐ Psalm 29:11 The LORD will give strength to His people; The LORD will bless His people with peace.

☐ Psalm 45:1-2 My heart overflows with a good theme; I address my verses to the King; My tongue is the pen of a ready writer. You are fairer than the sons of men; Grace is poured upon Your lips; Therefore God has blessed You forever.

☐ Psalm 46:1-3 God is our refuge and strength, a very present help in trouble. Therefore we will not fear, though the earth should change and though the mountains slip into the heart of the sea; though its waters roar and foam, though the mountains quake at its swelling pride.

☐ Psalm 47:1-4 O clap your hands, all peoples; Shout to God with the voice of joy. For the LORD Most High is to be feared, A great King over all the earth. He subdues peoples under us And nations under our feet. He chooses our inheritance for us, The glory of Jacob whom He loves.

☐ Psalm 48:1 Great is the LORD, and greatly to be praised, in the city of our God, His holy mountain.

☐ Psalm 49:3-5 My mouth will speak wisdom, and the meditation of my heart will be understanding. I will incline my ear to a proverb; I will express my riddle on the harp. Why should I fear in days of adversity, When the iniquity of my foes surrounds me.

☐ Psalm 50:14-15 Offer to God a sacrifice of thanksgiving And pay your vows to the Most High; Call upon Me in the day of trouble; I shall rescue you, and you will honor Me.

☐ Psalm 73:23-26 Nevertheless I am continually with You; You have taken hold of my right hand. With Your counsel You will guide me, And afterward receive me to glory. Whom have I in heaven but You? And besides You, I desire nothing on earth. My flesh and my heart may fail, but God is the strength of my heart and my portion forever.

☐ Psalm 81:10 I, the LORD, am your God, Who brought you up from the land of Egypt; Open your mouth wide and I will fill it.

☐ Psalm 82:3-4 Vindicate the weak and fatherless; Do justice to the afflicted and destitute. Rescue the weak and needy; Deliver them out of the hand of the wicked.

☐ Psalm 84:9-12 Behold our shield, O God, and look upon the face of Your anointed. For a day in Your courts is better than a thousand outside. I would rather stand at the threshold of the house of my God than dwell in the tents of wickedness. For the LORD God is a sun and shield; The LORD gives grace and glory; No good thing does He withhold from those who walk uprightly. O LORD of hosts, How blessed is the woman who trusts in You!

☐ Psalm 93:1-2 The LORD reigns, He is clothed with majesty; The LORD has clothed and girded Himself with strength; Indeed, the world is firmly established, it will not be moved. Your throne is established from of old; You are from everlasting.

☐ Psalm 96:7-9 Ascribe to the LORD, O families of the peoples, Ascribe to the LORD glory and strength. Ascribe to the LORD the glory of His name; Bring an offering and come into His courts. Worship the LORD in holy attire; Tremble before Him, all the earth.

☐ Psalm 97:8-12 Zion heard this and was glad, And the daughters of Judah have rejoiced Because of Your judgments, O LORD. For You are the LORD Most High over all the earth; You are exalted far above all gods. Hate evil, you who love the LORD, Who preserves the souls of His godly ones; He delivers them from the hand of the wicked. Light is sown like seed for the righteous And gladness for the upright in heart. Be glad in the LORD, you righteous ones, And give thanks to His holy name.

☐ Psalm 98:1-4 O sing to the LORD a new song, For He has done wonderful things, His right hand and His holy arm have gained the victory for Him. The LORD has made known His salvation; He has revealed His righteousness in the sight of the nations. He has remembered His loving kindness and His faithfulness to the house of Israel; All the ends of the earth have seen the salvation of our God. Shout joyfully to the LORD, all the earth; Break forth and sing for joy and sing praises.

☐ Psalm 101:1-3 I will sing of loving kindness and justice, To You, O LORD, I will sing praises. I will give heed to the blameless way. When will You come to me? I will walk within my house in the integrity of my heart. I will set no worthless thing before my eyes; I hate the work of those who fall away; It shall not fasten its grip on me.

☐ Psalm 112:4-7 Light arises in the darkness for the upright; she is gracious and compassionate and righteous. It is well with the woman who is gracious and lends; He will maintain her cause in judgment. For she will never be shaken; the righteous will be remembered forever. She will not fear evil tidings; her heart is steadfast, trusting in the LORD.

☐ Psalm 122:6-7 Pray for the peace of Jerusalem: "May they prosper who love you. May peace be within your walls, and prosperity within your palaces."

☐ Psalm 127:1-2 Unless the LORD builds the house, they labor in vain who build it; Unless the LORD guards the city, The watchman keeps awake in vain. It is vain for you to rise up early, To retire late, To eat the bread of painful labors; For He gives to His beloved even in her sleep.

☐ Psalm 128:1-2 How blessed is everyone who fears the LORD, Who walks in His ways. When you shall eat of the fruit of your hands, You will be happy and it will be well with you.

☐ Psalm 133:1-3 Behold, how good and how pleasant it is for sisters to dwell together in unity! It is like the precious oil upon the head, Coming down upon the beard, Even Aaron's beard, Coming down upon the edge of his robes. It is like the dew of Hermon Coming down upon the mountains of Zion; for there the LORD commanded the blessing—life forever.

☐ Psalm 134:1-3 Behold, bless the LORD, all servants of the LORD, Who serve by night in the house of the LORD! Lift up your hands to the sanctuary and bless the LORD. May the LORD bless you from Zion, He who made heaven and earth.

Psalms of Lament

☐ Psalm 3:3-5 But You, O Lord, are a shield about me, my glory, and the One who lifts my head. I was crying to the Lord with my voice, And He answered me from His holy mountain. I lay down and slept; I awoke, for the Lord sustains me.

☐ Psalm 4:3-5 But know that the Lord has set apart the godly woman for Himself; The Lord hears when I call to Him. Tremble, and do not sin; Meditate in your heart upon your bed, and be still. Offer the sacrifices of righteousness, and trust in the Lord.

☐ Psalm 6:6-9 I am weary with my sighing; every night I make my bed swim, I dissolve my couch with my tears. My eye has wasted away with grief; it has become old because of all my adversaries. Depart from me, all you who do iniquity, for the Lord has heard the voice of my weeping. The Lord has heard my supplication, the Lord receives my prayer.

☐ Psalm 7:1 O Lord my God, in You I have taken refuge; save me from all those who pursue me, and deliver me.

☐ Psalm 9:9-10 The Lord also will be a stronghold for the oppressed, a stronghold in times of trouble; and those who know Your name will put their trust in You, For You, O Lord, have not forsaken those who seek You.

☐ Psalm 10:17-18 O Lord, You have heard the desire of the humble; You will strengthen their heart, You will incline Your ear. To vindicate the orphan and the oppressed, so that man who is of the earth will no longer cause terror.

☐ Psalm 13:5-6 But I have trusted in Your lovingkindness; my heart shall rejoice in Your salvation. I will sing to the Lord, because He has dealt bountifully with me.

☐ Psalm 17:3,8 You have tried my heart; You have visited me by night; You have tested me and You find nothing; I have purposed that my mouth will not transgress. Keep me as the apple of Your eye; hide me in the shadow of Your wings.

☐ Psalm 22:9-11 Yet You are He who brought me forth from the womb; You made me trust when upon my mother's breasts. Upon You I was cast from birth; You have been my God from my mother's womb. Be not far from me, for trouble is near; for there is none to help.

☐ Psalm 25:6-7 Remember, O Lord, Your compassion and Your lovingkindnesses, for they have been from of old. Do not remember the sins of my youth or my transgressions; according to Your lovingkindness remember me, for Your goodness' sake, O Lord.

☐ Psalm 26:1-3 Vindicate me, O Lord, for I have walked in my integrity, and I have trusted in the Lord without wavering. Examine me, O Lord, and try me; test my mind and my heart. For Your lovingkindness is before my eyes, and I have walked in Your truth.

☐ Psalm 27:1,4 The Lord is my light and my salvation; whom shall I fear? The Lord is the defense of my life; whom shall I dread? One thing I have asked from the Lord, that I shall seek: That I may dwell in the house of the Lord all the days of my life, to behold the beauty of the Lord and to meditate in His temple.

☐ Psalm 31:23-24 O love the Lord, all you His godly ones! The Lord preserves the faithful and fully recompenses the proud doer. Be strong and let your heart take courage, all you who hope in the Lord.

☐ Psalm 51:6-7 Behold, You desire truth in the innermost being, and in the hidden part You will make me know wisdom. Purify me with hyssop, and I shall be clean; wash me, and I shall be whiter than snow.

☐ Psalm 54:6-7 Willingly I will sacrifice to You; I will give thanks to Your name, O Lord, for it is good. For He has delivered me from all trouble, and my eye has looked with satisfaction upon my enemies.

☐ Psalm 60:11-12 O give us help against the adversary, for deliverance by man is in vain. Through God we shall do valiantly, and it is He who will tread down our adversaries.

☐ Psalm 61:1-3 Hear my cry, O God; give heed to my prayer. From the end of the earth I call to You when my heart is faint; lead me to the rock that is higher than I. For You have been a refuge for me, a tower of strength against the enemy.

☐ Psalm 64:9-10 Then all women will fear, and they will declare the work of God, and will consider what He has done. The righteous woman will be glad in the Lord and will take refuge in Him; and all the upright in heart will glory.

☐ Psalm 70:4-5 Let all who seek You rejoice and be glad in You; and let those who love Your salvation say continually, "Let God be magnified." But I am afflicted and needy; hasten to me, O God! You are my help and my deliverer; O Lord, do not delay.

☐ Psalm 77:1-3 My voice rises to God, and I will cry aloud; my voice rises to God, and He will hear me. In the day of my trouble I sought the Lord; in the night my hand was stretched out without weariness; my soul refused to be comforted. When I remember God, then I am disturbed; when I sigh, then my spirit grows faint.

☐ Psalm 79:13 So we Your people and the sheep of Your pasture will give thanks to You forever; to all generations we will tell of Your praise.

☐ Psalm 83:18 That they may know that You alone, whose name is the Lord, are the Most High over all the earth.

☐ Psalm 86:5-7 For You, Lord, are good, and ready to forgive, and abundant in lovingkindness to all who call upon You. Give ear, O Lord, to my prayer; and give heed to the voice of my supplications! In the day of my trouble I shall call upon You, for You will answer me.

☐ Psalm 88:1-2 O Lord, the God of my salvation, I have cried out by day and in the night before You. Let my prayer come before You; incline Your ear to my cry!

☐ Psalm 120:1-2,7 In my trouble I cried to the Lord, and He answered me. Deliver my soul, O Lord, from lying lips, from a deceitful tongue. I am for peace, but when I speak, they are for war.

☐ Psalm 123:2 Behold, as the eyes of servants look to the hand of their master, as the eyes of a maid to the hand of her mistress, so our eyes look to the Lord our God, until He is gracious to us.

☐ Psalm 137:4-6 How can we sing the Lord's song in a foreign land? If I forget you, O Jerusalem, may my right hand forget her skill. May my tongue cling to the roof of my mouth if I do not remember you, if I do not exalt Jerusalem above my chief joy.

☐ Psalm 142:1-3,7 I cry aloud with my voice to the Lord; I make supplication with my voice to the Lord. I pour out my complaint before Him; I declare my trouble before Him. When my spirit was overwhelmed within me, You knew my path. In the way where I walk they have hidden a trap for me. Bring my soul out of prison, so that I may give thanks to Your name; the righteous will surround me, for You will deal bountifully with me.

☐ Psalm 143:8 Let me hear Your lovingkindness in the morning; for I trust in You; teach me the way in which I should walk; for to You I lift up my soul.

Psalms of Thanksgiving

☐ Psalm 8:3-4 When I consider Your heavens, the work of Your fingers, the moon and the stars, which You have ordained; what is woman that You take thought of her, and the daughter of man that You care for her?

☐ Psalm 16:6-8 The lines have fallen to me in pleasant places; indeed, my heritage is beautiful to me. I will bless the Lord who has counseled me; indeed, my mind instructs me in the night. I have set the Lord continually before me; because He is at my right hand, I will not be shaken.

☐ Psalm 23:1-3 The Lord is my shepherd, I shall not want. He makes me lie down in green pastures; He leads me beside quiet waters. He restores my soul; He guides me in the paths of righteousness for His name's sake.

☐ Psalm 34:1-4 I will bless the Lord at all times; His praise shall continually be in my mouth. My soul will make its boast in the Lord; the humble will hear it and rejoice. O magnify the Lord with me, and let us exalt His name together. I sought the Lord, and He answered me, and delivered me from all my fears.

☐ Psalm 63:1,8 O God, You are my God; I shall seek You earnestly; my soul thirsts for You, my flesh yearns for You, in a dry and weary land where there is no water. My soul clings to You; Your right hand upholds me.

☐ Psalm 66:1-2,4 Shout joyfully to God, all the earth; sing the glory of His name; make His praise glorious. "All the earth will worship You, and will sing praises to You; they will sing praises to Your name."

☐ Psalm 67:1-3 God be gracious to us and bless us, and cause His face to shine upon us that Your way may be known on the earth, Your salvation among all nations. Let the peoples praise You, O God; let all the peoples praise You.

☐ Psalm 75:1 We give thanks to You, O God, we give thanks, for Your name is near; women declare Your wondrous works.

☐ Psalm 92:1-2 It is good to give thanks to the Lord and to sing praises to Your name, O Most High; to declare Your lovingkindness in the morning and Your faithfulness by night.

☐ Psalm 92:12-15 The righteous woman will flourish like the palm tree, she will grow like a cedar in Lebanon. Planted in the house of the Lord, they will flourish in the courts of our God. They will still yield fruit in old age; they shall be full of sap and very green, to declare that the Lord is upright; He is my rock, and there is no unrighteousness in Him.

☐ Psalm 95:1-3 O come, let us sing for joy to the Lord, let us shout joyfully to the rock of our salvation. Let us come before His presence with thanksgiving, let us shout joyfully to Him with psalms. For the Lord is a great God and a great King above all gods.

☐ Psalm 95:6-7 Come, let us worship and bow down, let us kneel before the Lord our Maker. For He is our God, and we are the people of His pasture and the sheep of His hand.

☐ Psalm 100:1-5 Shout joyfully to the Lord, all the earth. Serve the Lord with gladness; come before Him with joyful singing. Know that the Lord Himself is God; it is He who has made us, and not we ourselves; we are His people and the sheep of His pasture. Enter His gates with thanksgiving and His courts with praise. Give thanks to Him, bless His name. For the Lord is good; His lovingkindness is everlasting and His faithfulness to all generations.

☐ Psalm 103:1-5 Bless the Lord, O my soul, and all that is within me, bless His holy name. Bless the Lord, O my soul, and forget none of His benefits; Who pardons all your iniquities, Who heals all your diseases; Who redeems your life from the pit, Who crowns you with lovingkindness and compassion; Who satisfies your years with good things, So that your youth is renewed like the eagle.

☐ Psalm 103:11-13 For as high as the heavens are above the earth, so great is His lovingkindness toward those who fear Him. As far as the east is from the west, so far has He removed our transgressions from us. Just as a mother has compassion on her children, so the Lord has compassion on those who fear Him.

☐ Psalm 103:14-16 For He Himself knows our frame; He is mindful that we are but dust. As for woman, her days are like grass; as a flower of the field, so she flourishes. When the wind has passed over it, it is no more, and its place acknowledges it no longer.

☐ Psalm 103:17-18 But the loving kindness of the Lord is from everlasting to everlasting on those who fear Him, and His righteousness to children's children, to those who keep His covenant and remember His precepts to do them.

☐ Psalm 107:1-2 Oh give thanks to the Lord, for He is good, for His lovingkindness is everlasting. Let the redeemed of the Lord say so, whom He has redeemed from the hand of the adversary.

☐ Psalm 107:8-9 Let them give thanks to the Lord for His lovingkindness, and for His wonders to the daughters of women! For He has satisfied the thirsty soul, and the hungry soul He has filled with what is good.

☐ Psalm 111:1-4,10 Praise the Lord! I will give thanks to the Lord with all my heart, in the company of the upright and in the assembly. Great are the works of the Lord; they are studied by all who delight in them. Splendid and majestic is

His work, and His righteousness endures forever. He has made His wonders to be remembered; the Lord is gracious and compassionate. The fear of the Lord is the beginning of wisdom; a good understanding have all those who do His commandments; His praise endures forever.

☐ Psalm 113:1-4 Praise the Lord! Praise, O servants of the Lord, praise the name of the Lord. Blessed be the name of the Lord from this time forth and forever. From the rising of the sun to its setting the name of the Lord is to be praised. The Lord is high above all nations; His glory is above the heavens.

☐ Psalm 116:1-2 I love the Lord, because He hears my voice and my supplications. Because He has inclined His ear to me, therefore I shall call upon Him as long as I live.

☐ Psalm 124:6-8 Blessed be the Lord, Who has not given us to be torn by their teeth. Our soul has escaped as a bird out of the snare of the trapper; the snare is broken and we have escaped. Our help is in the name of the Lord, Who made heaven and earth.

☐ Psalm 138:3,8 On the day I called, You answered me; You made me bold with strength in my soul. The Lord will accomplish what concerns me; Your loving kindness, O Lord, is everlasting; do not forsake the works of Your hands.

☐ Psalm 146:5-9 How blessed is she whose help is the God of Jacob, whose hope is in the Lord her God, who made heaven and earth, the sea and all that is in them; Who keeps faith forever; Who executes justice for the oppressed; Who gives food to the hungry. The Lord sets the prisoners free. The Lord opens the eyes of the blind; the Lord raises up those who are bowed down; the Lord loves the righteous; the Lord protects the strangers; He supports the fatherless and the widow, but He thwarts the way of the wicked.

☐ Psalm 150:1-6 Praise the Lord! Praise God in His sanctuary; praise Him in His mighty expanse. Praise Him for His mighty deeds; praise Him according to His excellent greatness. Praise Him with trumpet sound; praise Him with harp and lyre. Praise Him with timbrel and dancing; praise Him with stringed instruments and pipe. Praise Him with loud cymbals; praise Him with resounding cymbals. Let everything that has breath praise the Lord. Praise the Lord!